CULTURAL JOURNEYS

TRADITIONS FROM THE
CARIBBEAN

Paul Dash

WAYLAND

CULTURAL JOURNEYS

Wh'appen, man? (A Caribbean greeting.)

TRADITIONS FROM AFRICA

TRADITIONS FROM THE CARIBBEAN

TRADITIONS FROM CHINA

TRADITIONS FROM INDIA

Cover: Two children from St Kitts wearing colourful carnival costumes.
Title page: A Grenadan fisherman displays his catch – two giant, wriggling lobsters.
Contents page: These sisters are from the Caribbean island of Antigua.
Index: A girl sells papayas from a stall in the Dominican Republic.

Series editor: Katie Orchard
Book editor: Alison Cooper
Designers: Tim Mayer/Mark Whitchurch
Production controller: Carol Stevens

First published in 1998 by Wayland Publishers Limited
61 Western Road, Hove
East Sussex, BN3 1JD, England

Find Wayland on the Internet at http://www.wayland.co.uk

British Library Cataloguing in Publication Data
Dash, Paul
Traditions from the Caribbean. – (Cultural journeys)
1. Caribbean Area – Social life and customs – Juvenile literature
I. Title
390'.09729

ISBN 0 7502 2186 0

Typeset by Mayer Media/ Mark Whitchurch Art & Design
Printed and bound by Eurografica, Vicenza, Italy.

Picture Acknowledgements:
Ace 4–5 (Ronald Toms); Action Plus 37 (Stephane Mantey); Bruce Coleman 14; Eye Ubiquitous 13 (David Cumming), 27 (Tim Page), 34 (David Cumming), 40 (Bruce Adams); Getty Images *cover border* (Kristin Finnegan), *title page* (Oliver Benn), 7 (Bob Krist), 9 (Doug Armand), 17 (Sylvain Grandadam), 29 (Oliver Benn), 31 (Bob Thomas), 32 (Bob Krist), 39 (Bob Thomas); Robert Harding *cover main pic* (Larsen Collinge), 18 (Larsen Collinge), 19, 30 (Tomlinson); Hutchison 10 (J. Highet), 12 (N. Durrell McKenna), 15 (John Wright), 16 (Jeremy Horner), 48 (N. Durrell McKenna); Image Bank *contents page* (Amanda Adey); Impact 28 (Mitch de Faria), 38 (Tom Webster), 42 (Mohammed Ansar); Panos 6 (Liba Taylor), 8 (Guy Mansfield), 11 (Sean Sprague), 22 (Marc French), 26 (Marc French), 33 (Marc French), 35 (Marc French), 36 (Jean-Leo Dugast), 41 (Marc French); South American Pictures 24 (Roland Pujol); Trip 23 (D. Saunders), 25 (B. Swanson); Wayland Picture Library 21 (Roland Pujol). The map on page 5 is by Peter Bull. All border artwork for the interest boxes is by Pip Adams. The line illustrations for the story are by Helen Holroyd.

CONTENTS

ISLANDS IN THE SUN

Welcome to the Caribbean. For hundreds of years, people have come from different parts of the world to settle in these lush, tropical islands. Some Caribbean families have ancestors who came from Asia, Africa and Europe.

▼ Fishermen in Tobago pull in their nets, as other islanders watch to see how many fish they have caught.

The first settlers sailed here in small boats from the American mainland. They were from three main peoples – the Carib, the Arawak and the Ciboney. The Caribbean Sea is named after the Carib people.

These first settlers, and those who came after them, brought with them new foods, new styles of clothing, and their own ways of celebrating and having fun. Today, life in the Caribbean is an exciting mixture of these different traditions.

▼ **The Caribbean Sea lies between the USA and South America. It contains many islands of different sizes.**

USA

BAHAMAS

CAICOS AND
TURKS ISLANDS

The Caribbean's place in the world

CUBA

GREATER ANTILLES

HISPANIOLA

HAITI   DOMINICAN
REPUBLIC

JAMAICA

ST THOMAS
VIRGIN
ISLANDS
PUERTO
RICO

ST CROIX

LEEWARD ISLANDS

ANGUILLA
ST MARTIN
BARBUDA
ANTIGUA

ST KITTS
NEVIS
MONSERRAT

GUADELOUPE

DOMINICA

MARTINIQUE

LESSER ANTILLES

CARIBBEAN SEA

DUTCH ANTILLES

ARUBA
BONAIRE
CURAÇAO

ST LUCIA
ST
VINCENT

BARBADOS

WINDWARD ISLANDS

GRENADA

TOBAGO

TRINIDAD

SOUTH AMERICA

New Arrivals

The first European explorer to visit the Caribbean was Christopher Columbus. In 1492 he set sail from Spain, hoping to reach India, but instead he landed in the Bahamas. Columbus and the Europeans who arrived after him treated the local people with great cruelty and soon took control of the whole region.

The Caribbean became important to Europeans because the islands were very fertile. The Europeans brought thousands of people from Africa to work as slaves on plantations, growing sugar-cane, cotton and other crops.

In the nineteenth century slavery came to an end. Many former slaves would no longer work in the fields, so people from India were taken to work in the Caribbean plantations instead. They were badly paid and their lives were very hard. People from China and Syria also settled in some Caribbean countries.

▼ These children on the island of St Vincent have Carib and African ancestors.

After the Second World War (1939–45), more workers were needed in Europe, the USA and Canada. Many Caribbean people left their island homes and settled in big cities overseas. They took with them their different customs and skills.

▲ **This man in Dominica is using traditional materials – cane, reeds and grasses – to weave baskets.**

CARIBBEAN FOOD

There are many different styles of cooking around the Caribbean. European, African and Asian settlers all brought to the islands their own ways of preparing food. Over the years, their traditional cooking has mixed with Arawak and Carib cooking to create a rich mixture of Caribbean dishes.

Many of the foods that are eaten in the Caribbean are grown locally. The hot, moist climate is ideal for growing a huge range of fruits and vegetables. Root vegetables are important in Caribbean cookery. Cassava comes from America, but sweet potatoes and yams were brought to the Caribbean from Africa. These vegetables are usually boiled, although sweet potatoes are sometimes roasted. They are often used to make tasty soups and stews.

▼ **This Jamaican farmer has just picked these crisp lettuces.**

Root vegetables ▶ such as dasheene, yams and sweet potatoes are on sale at this market in Grenada.

8

Delicious Fruits

Star apples, sugar apples, custard apples and breadfruit are just a few of the many fruits that grow in the Caribbean. As the fruits ripen on the trees in the warm sunshine, colourful birds peck at their sweet flesh.

Some delicious fruits, such as pawpaws (which are also called papayas) and guavas, are native to the Caribbean, but others were brought to the region by settlers. Mangoes were brought to the Caribbean from India. These colourful, juicy fruits have a similar taste to a ripe peach. Ackees were originally grown in Africa. They grow in pods, which burst open when the fruit is ripe. If an ackee is not ripe, it can be poisonous.

Many people enjoy drinking the milk and eating the soft flesh of a fresh coconut. Coconuts are coated with a thick fibre that keeps the milk inside cool.

▼ **Fruit piled high on a farm stall in Jamaica. The fruits with the black centres are ackees.**

▲ A market trader in Haiti fries bananas to sell on her food stall.

Cash Crops

Not all the crops that are grown in the Caribbean provide food for the islanders. Many are grown to be sold to other countries. These crops are called cash crops. Bananas are the main cash crop in the Caribbean, and the largest banana crop comes from St Lucia. Sugar-cane is an important crop for Jamaica and Cuba. Coffee and some spices are important cash crops, too.

To make a Caribbean fruit salad, look in the supermarket for pineapples, guavas, passionfruit, papayas and mangoes. Ask an adult to help you cut up the fruit into bite-sized pieces. Mix all the fruit together and soak it in orange juice. Serve the fruit salad with cream or yoghurt.

This boy is checking coffee ▶ plants in Jamaica.

▼ A cane-cutter at work in the fields, in the Dominican Republic.

Feasting on Fish

▼A fisherman sells his catch on the beach in Tobago.

Fish is eaten everywhere in the Caribbean. Swordfish, red snapper and flying fish are favourites. Saltfish patties are popular on some islands, such as Jamaica.

Caribbean Favourites

▲ Jerk pork is cooked in the traditional way – outdoors over a fire – in Jamaica.

Cou cou is a dish that came from Africa. It is made from ground corn and looks a bit like mashed potato. Rice-and-peas is another popular dish, which is similar to the bean meals that are eaten in parts of Africa.

Curries and flat breads called *rotis* and *chapatis* were introduced by settlers from India. Many other spicy dishes in the Caribbean also have a South Asian origin. But jerk pork, a spicy Jamaican dish, is based on an Arawak way of preparing meat. The pork is seasoned and spiced, and then cooked over an open grill, much like a barbecue.

Caribbean people who have left the islands have introduced their favourite dishes to other countries. Foods such as jerk pork, *roti* dishes, rice-and-peas, and mangoes are now enjoyed by people all over the world.

CLOTHES AND COSTUME

Most people in the Caribbean wear Western-style clothing. Dresses and shirts made of lightweight cotton help them to keep cool in the warm, tropical climate. The peoples who came to live in the Caribbean in the past brought their own styles of clothing to the region, and adapted them to suit their new way of life. Colourful traditional clothing is still worn at special events such as festivals.

The women of Martinique make costumes which are worn at special times, such as national days. Their richly-coloured dresses, bright headscarves and gold jewellery are similar to those worn by women in Ghana and other parts of West Africa.

These women wearing ▶ traditional dress are from Martinique. They wear clothes like these only on special occasions.

▼ Islanders unload a boat in St Lucia. Their light cotton clothes help them to keep cool while they work.

Carnival Costumes

Very special costumes are worn at Carnival in Trinidad. Costume-makers use felt, paper, cloth, bits of plastic and other materials to make their stunning carnival outfits. Some costumes are so huge that they have to be put on wheels so that they can be taken through the streets. Some tell a story in shapes, signs, pictures or even words. Carnival costumes cost a lot of money and can take a long time to make. The people taking part in the celebrations don't mind too much because they enjoy wearing them.

At the Surinam carnival some women wear headscarves called *angisas* as part of their costumes. *Angisas* are similar to the headscarves worn in Africa and Martinique. They can be folded into shapes that have special meanings. For example, if a headscarf has one or more points sticking out, it means that the woman wearing it is angry.

Amazing costumes are worn ▶ at many Caribbean festivals. Here, a performer is entertaining the crowds in Barbados.

◀ These children are taking part in a carnival competition in St Kitts. Their costumes are made from feathers and strips of brightly-coloured cloth.

18

Carnival Around the World

Breath-taking costumes can be seen whenever Caribbean carnivals are held in cities around the world. Each year, Caribbean people take to the streets of Amsterdam, New York, Toronto and London in dazzling processions. In many countries, fashion designers from the Caribbean are also adding their sense of colour and fun to everyday clothes.

Try creating a carnival costume that would make you stand out in the crowd. First, choose a theme, such as nature. Then, let your imagination run wild! Use bright colours and as many different types of material as you can.

▼ **A Caribbean carnival brings colour to the streets of Notting Hill in London.**

Uniforms

Many of the uniforms that are worn in the Caribbean were introduced to the region by Europeans. The police uniforms worn on St Lucia and many other islands, for example, were introduced by the British. In the old days, policemen often wore large hats which were lined with cork. The cork linings helped to protect their heads from the fierce heat of the sun.

MUSIC AND DANCE

People who were taken to the Caribbean as slaves danced and made music as a way of showing pride in their traditional way of life. Gradually, their traditions mixed with those of other settlers and new forms of dance and music developed.

Calypso

Calypso started in Trinidad, but it is now heard everywhere in the Caribbean and in many other countries. Calypsos often tell stories, and the most popular ones are those that make people laugh. They might be funny stories about important people, such as presidents and prime ministers, or silly stories about smelly goats, mad dogs or bad-tempered bulls. With their catchy rhythms, calypsos are part of the fun and excitement of Carnival.

▼ Caribbean people enjoy street festivals and parties. These people are playing music and having fun on the streets of Haiti.

Reggae

Reggae comes from Jamaica. It was made popular by Bob Marley, who became famous all over the world. Reggae has an unusual beat, which makes it sound different from other music. Many people enjoy dancing to it, creating their own movements and dance steps.

▲ Bob Marley sings at a concert. Thousands of people came to hear his reggae performances. He died in 1981, but his music is still popular.

Drums

The sound of the drum is important in Caribbean music. Even very young children enjoy tapping rhythms on their thighs, or on tables and tin cans. Some of the finest drummers come from Cuba. They are famous for playing the bongo and conga drums. The bongos are a pair of small drums that are joined together. The drummers hold them between their knees and play them with their hands and fingers. The conga is a barrel drum. It is played with the fingers and hands, too.

Try making a drum set from scrap materials. Collect cans and boxes of various shapes and sizes and tap them with thin sticks or your fingers and hands. See how many sounds and rhythms you can make.

▼ **These Cuban drummers are playing a mixture of African and Cuban music.**

Steel Pans

Steel pans are often used in calypso music. They are ideal for Carnival because they are light and their sound carries a long way through streets crowded with noisy revellers. Steel pans were first made in Trinidad, from unwanted oil drums cut to different sizes. To make the steel pans, the bases of the 'pans' were heated over a fire and beaten into a basin shape. Circular patterns were then punched into the curved base, to produce all the different notes.

This man from Tobago is ▶ playing the bass pans in a steel band. The steel pan is the national instrument of Trinidad and Tobago.

Dance

Dance plays an important part in voodoo ceremonies. Voodoo is a religion that is followed by some Caribbean people, especially in Haiti. Here, people dance to the sound of special drums, rattles and bamboo pipes at religious services. During the services, dancers become possessed by the spirits of the gods, or *loas*, and move in special ways.

▼ This man from Haiti is doing a special voodoo dance.

Limbo Dancing

Limbo dancing is popular on many Caribbean islands. The dancers take turns to bend over backwards and wriggle under a bar, like the bar on a high jump. The bar is set lower each time, to see which dancer can squeeze through the smallest space. Limbo dancing is very difficult to do, and the dancers need to have strong legs. The best dancers can wriggle under a bar set just 25 cm above the ground.

Caribbean people of all ages ▶ enjoy dancing. These young dancers are from Cuba.

RELIGION AND FESTIVALS

There are people of many different faiths in the Caribbean. Temples and mosques can be found alongside Christian churches. Each religion has its own festivals and special occasions which bring colour and excitement to the islands.

Carnival

The best-known Caribbean festival is the Trinidad Carnival. Carnival shows how the different peoples who have settled in the region have created their own Caribbean traditions. The festival was introduced by European Christians, and it takes place just before Lent. Much of the music and dance is of African origin. Settlers from India added the bright colours and large costumes that are now a vital part of the celebrations.

Dyed feathers, shiny cloth ▶ and gold trimmings have been used to make this woman's spectacular costume.

▼ Four boys wait to join the procession on Children's Day at the Trinidad Carnival.

Festival Time

Many other carnivals and festivals take place on different islands and at different times of the year. Hosein is another important festival that takes place in Trinidad. This festival was started by people from India, and it is famous for the big floats that are carried through the streets.

▼ **Dancers and drummers perform on a colourful float in the Pirates' Week parade on Grand Cayman, in the Cayman Islands.**

You could hold your own Caribbean carnival. Design and make some costumes – you could even design a float. Try making up some calypsos about funny things that have happened to you. Make up some music and dance to the rhythm of the drums.

In Barbados people celebrate the end of the sugar-cane harvest with a festival called Crop Over. It is similar to Carnival in many ways – people take part in huge processions and enjoy music and dancing.

Pierrot Grenade is a festival that started in St Kitts. 'Pierrot' is the French word for a clown with a painted white face and tall, pointed hat. At Pierrot Grenade people dress up as pierrots and dance in the streets. The festival was later introduced to Trinidad by settlers from St Kitts.

▲ **Dancers with whistles and drums beat the rhythm of a traditional dance, at the *Junkanoo* Festival in the Bahamas.**

Christianity

When Europeans came to settle in the Caribbean, they brought their Christian faith and traditions with them. Sometimes, it was quite difficult to adapt their traditional celebrations to their new way of life. Barbados, for example, is a country that has temperatures of 25 °C and higher throughout the year. Snow is never seen there. But Europeans were used to celebrating Christmas when it was cold and snowy. So, many years ago, each Christmas Eve, people would take buckets of white dust from the local quarries and spread the dust thinly around their homes, so that they could have a white Christmas.

▼ These girls from St Lucia are dressed for their First Communion. Roman Catholic girls all over the world wear white dresses for this ceremony.

▲ **Christians leave a church in Jamaica at the end of a service. Many Caribbean churches, like this one, were built by the British.**

Today, Christian hymns ring out across the Caribbean each Sunday. In the churches, the people sing and play guitars, cymbals, drums, organs and other instruments. A similar energy and joy can be found wherever Caribbean people worship in churches around the world.

Rastafarianism

The Rastafarians are an important group in the Caribbean. Their religion began in Jamaica in the 1920s. Rastafarians believe that Haile Selassie, the emperor of Ethiopia in the mid-twentieth century, was a god. Ethiopia is a very special place for them. Today, many people in the Caribbean, Britain, the USA and elsewhere are Rastafarians.

▼ A Rastafarian man with his daughter. Many Rastafarians have long hair which they wear in a style called 'dreadlocks'.

African Influences

Other less well-known faiths are also found in the Caribbean. The people of Haiti worship voodoo gods, or *loas*. Voodoo is based on a mixture of African and Catholic beliefs.

Many African religions and ways of worship were brought to the Caribbean by slaves. In Cuba, for example, flags, drawings and special altars, or *nkisi*, are used in some services. This type of service began in the Congo in central Africa and was taken to Cuba by slaves.

SPORTS AND GAMES

Many of the world's best sportsmen and sportswomen were born in the Caribbean. Cuba, Jamaica, Puerto Rico, and Trinidad and Tobago are just some of the Caribbean countries that have produced Olympic medal-winners. They have achieved success in various sports, including track and field athletics, boxing and swimming. Caribbean basketball players and footballers play for top teams in the USA, Canada and Europe.

▼ **Teenagers in the Dominican Republic spend an evening playing basketball.**

◄ Deon Burton, a Jamaican footballer, plays for his country in a match against El Salvador.

Cricket

On islands that used to be ruled by Britain, one of the most popular sports is cricket. Cricket was introduced to the Caribbean during the nineteenth century, and it became very popular amongst the local people. After the Second World War, the West Indies became one of the best teams in the world. For many years they were the world champions.

Playing Games

Caribbean children spend a lot of time playing outdoors. One of the games they play is street tennis, which is a cross between lawn tennis and table tennis. They place a long piece of wood across the playing area and hit the ball backwards and forwards, over the wood.

Marble cricket is a version of cricket that can be played in small areas, such as gardens. In parts of the countryside in the Caribbean, children make their own balls for marble cricket from lumps of tar. When the sun is at its hottest and the road surfaces begin to melt, the children pull off small pieces of tar and roll them into a little ball. Then, they are ready to play.

To play marble cricket, you need 4–5 people for each team, some stumps, a bat and a ball. The people batting and bowling kneel on one knee, but they can stand up to run. Run between the stumps to score points. You are 'out' if a member of the other team catches the ball, or hits the stumps with the ball while you are running.

These boys from Barbados ▶ are playing beach cricket. Sometimes they have to wade into the sea to get the ball.

◀ These children are having fun on the swings in a play area in the Bahamas.

Looping the Loop

▲ **Two girls from St Lucia get in a tangle as they skip together.**

Another popular pastime in the Caribbean is kite-flying. People who are clever at flying kites can make them dive, spin and perform special tricks. Many of the best kites have a 'bull', or buzzer, which vibrates in the wind, making a loud noise. Some kites are called singing angels because they have lots of bulls which make different sounds.

Hide-and-seek

Some children like to play hide-and-seek in the sugar-cane fields. The best time to play this is when the canes are about 2 metres tall and it is easy to hide amongst them. This game can be a bit scary, because giant stinging centipedes lurk among the canes under layers of rubbish.

A boy in Kingston, Jamaica, ▶ **waits for the wind to catch his kite.**

41

STORY TIME

In the days before people had televisions, Caribbean families often spent their evenings telling stories. Many of these were traditional stories from the countries of their ancestors. The much-loved tales about Anancy, the cunning spiderman, for example, came originally from Africa. Other stories were told about people's own experiences. Ghost stories were very popular.

The story that follows is one that my father often told when I was a boy growing up in the Caribbean. It is based on something he actually saw.

▼ Evening in the Caribbean – the traditional time for telling tales.

THE DUPPY IN THE DARK
A Story Told By the Author's Father

One evening my father was walking through the countryside on his way home from work. It was getting late, and stars dusted the sky. There was a full moon.

As my father walked along he could see a long way in the cool, silvery light. The young sugar-cane plants, just a metre high, stretched away evenly, like a carpet, on either side. But the shadows of the trees that lined the lane were very, very dark.

My father wasn't really scared, but the sound of small animals scurrying in the bushes made him nervous. The wind sighed through a nearby pine forest. Bamboo leaves jingled in the breeze, like a chorus of tiny bells. Banana trees threw huge, dark shadows which bounced and danced on the country lane.

Keen to get home to his supper, my father took a short cut across the fields of a plantation. As he walked, he began to feel uneasy. When he was a boy, he had spent many happy hours exploring these fields for useful or unusual things: a lost kite or cricket ball, a colourful flower or a giant centipede. He knew the area well. But that night there was a strange feeling of unrest that he could not explain.

His shoes crunched the dried leaves underfoot. Sometimes he would slacken his pace to listen for other footsteps. But he was alone.

43

The Duppy in the Dark

The strange feeling would not go away. He quickened his pace, his hands buried deep in his pockets for comfort. Then, about 50 metres away, he saw something very odd. A dark shape stood out above the plants. It was directly in his path.

My father tried to work out what it was. It could not have been a bush; trees and shrubs had been cleared from the field. Neither was it a scarecrow; they were not needed on sugar plantations. Large wild animals did not exist in his country, and all farm animals would have been gathered in for the night. Children would not have dared to play in the field while the cane was still young. Mr Marshall, the farmer, would have chased them away. My father's heart began to thump against the walls of his chest.

The strange shape might be an 'outman', he thought. Escaped prisoners were called outmen by the local people. Children were always warned not to play amongst fully grown sugar-cane when a prisoner had escaped or when someone dangerous was on the run. At more than 3 metres high, mature cane plants were a perfect hiding place. But this cane was too young for someone to hide in.

My father had to keep calm and try not to show fear. His parents had always told him to control himself and be strong when harried by a madman or an angry dog. Now he realized that this was useful advice.

The Duppy in the Dark

He walked on slowly. The figure rose in little jerks to a standing position and began to move towards him. It seemed to look straight through him, swinging its arms with mechanical movements, like a wound-up toy.

My father, numb with fear, stopped walking. The figure made no sound, except for a strange hum which came with each step, as if walking was a real effort. No sound was made by its footsteps; it seemed to walk on cushions of air. It was a moment of sheer terror.

The figure walked up to him and, to his surprise, continued past him. Behind it, it left an awful smell, like rotting rubbish and smelly socks all rolled into one. Unable to tear himself away, my father turned slowly and followed the figure with his eyes. Then it vanished.

With that, my father came to his senses and ran as fast as he could to his mother's house. He banged and banged at the door, until she came to let him in. Beside himself with relief, he fell through the door like a sack of potatoes, in a deep faint.

TOPIC WEB

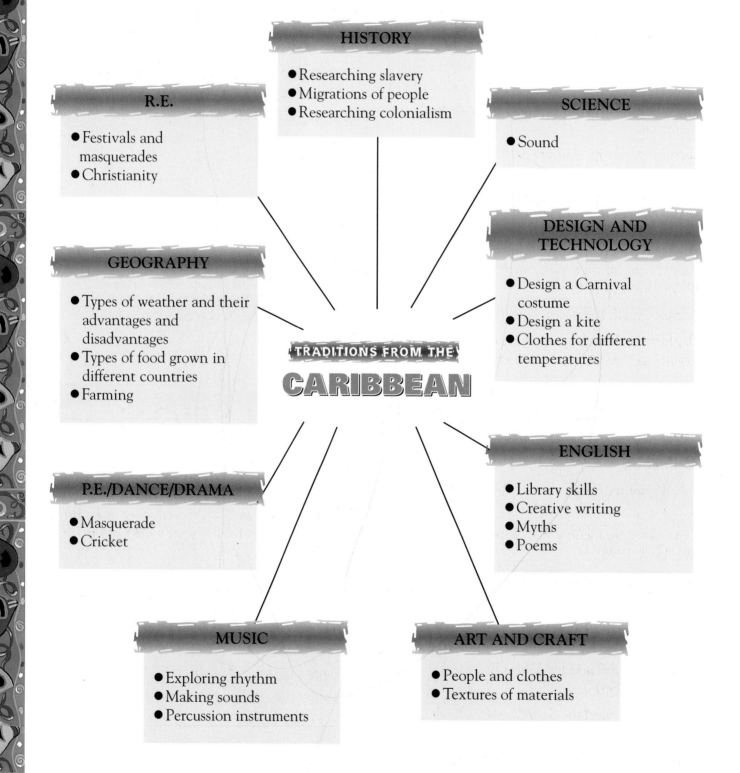

HISTORY
- Researching slavery
- Migrations of people
- Researching colonialism

R.E.
- Festivals and masquerades
- Christianity

SCIENCE
- Sound

GEOGRAPHY
- Types of weather and their advantages and disadvantages
- Types of food grown in different countries
- Farming

DESIGN AND TECHNOLOGY
- Design a Carnival costume
- Design a kite
- Clothes for different temperatures

TRADITIONS FROM THE CARIBBEAN

P.E./DANCE/DRAMA
- Masquerade
- Cricket

ENGLISH
- Library skills
- Creative writing
- Myths
- Poems

MUSIC
- Exploring rhythm
- Making sounds
- Percussion instruments

ART AND CRAFT
- People and clothes
- Textures of materials

GLOSSARY

Ancestors Family members who died long ago.

Arawaks One of the first peoples to settle in the Caribbean.

Calypso A song that tells a funny story.

Caribs One of the first peoples to settle in the Caribbean.

Cash crops Crops that are grown in large quantities to be sold, usually to other countries.

Duppy A Caribbean word for a ghost.

Floats Decorated vehicles that are used in carnival processions.

Lent A special time for Christians which lasts for 40 days just before Easter.

Patties Small, flat pies.

Plantations Very large farms, usually in tropical areas of the world, where cash crops are grown.

Possessed Taken over by strong spiritual forces. Followers of Voodoo believe that spirits speak through people who are possessed.

Roman Catholics Christians who are led by the Pope in Rome.

Root vegetables Vegetables such as potatoes, yams or carrots. The part that is eaten is the root, which grows underground.

Settlers People who go to live in a new country.

Slaves People who are owned by other people and forced to work for them.

Sugar-cane A tall plant that has juices which are rich in natural sugars.

Tropical Lying between the Tropics of Cancer and Capricorn. Tropical regions have hot, wet climates.

FURTHER INFORMATION

Non-fiction:

Cuba (Country Insights series) by Marion Morrison (Wayland, 1997)

A Flavour of the Caribbean by Linda Ilsley (Wayland, 1998)

Focus on the Caribbean by Cas Walker (Evans, 1995)

Jamaica (Country Insights series) by Alison Brownlie (Wayland, 1997)

The People of St Lucia by Alison Brownlie (Wayland, 1998)

Traditions Around the World series (Wayland, 1995)

World Religions by John Barker (Dorling Kindersley, 1997)

Fiction and Poetry:

African Tales by Saviour Pirotta (Wayland, 1998)

Can I Buy a Slice of Sky? Poems from Black, Asian and American Indian cultures, edited by Grace Nicholls (Hodder, 1996)

My Grandpa and the Sea by Katherine Orr (Carolrhoda Books Inc., 1990) Available from Worldaware, 31–35 Kirby Street, London EC1N 8TE.

Resource pack:

Jamaica, available from Channel 4 Schools.

INDEX

Page numbers in **bold** refer to photographs.